D0873814

by susanne strose

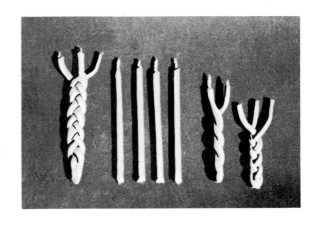

CANDLE-MAKING

**LITTLE
CRAFT BOOK
SERIES**

STERLING PUBLISHING CO., INC.   NEW YORK

Oak Tree Press   LONDON AND SYDNEY

Little Craft Book Series

Candle-Making
Coloring Papers
Nail Sculpture
Potato Printing

Translated by Paul Kuttner

Copyright © 1968 by
Sterling Publishing Co., Inc.
419 Park Avenue South, New York 10016.
British edition published in Great Britain and the Commonwealth by
The Oak Tree Press, Ltd., 116 Baker St., London, W.1.
The original edition was published in Germany under the title
"Kerzen" © 1967 by the Don Bosco Verlag, Munich, Germany.
Manufactured in the United States of America
All rights reserved
Library of Congress Catalog Card No.: 68-8759

Contents

Before You Begin

A candle is simply a cylinder of tallow, wax or other solid fat, containing a wick to give off light when burning. But besides giving light, a candle can be made to give color and fragrance and to give pleasure to the aesthetic sense by the addition of pleasing design. How to create and design candles is essentially what this book tells you.

Little is known of the history of candles, though we do know that they were used in Roman times. The modern candle probably evolved from the Middle Age custom of dipping cores of wood, rush or cords in household grease and burning these tallows as a source of light. In about 1825 the use of tallow, beeswax and vegetable wax—bayberry in the American colonies, candleberry in the East, and waxberry in South America—was supplemented by stearin. At about the same time, twisted cord was replaced by a plaited wick as the candle's core. Fifty years later, paraffin was added to the list of waxes used.

There are three main methods of making candles by hand: rolling sheets of beeswax around a wick, dipping the wick in hot wax, and pouring hot wax into a mould. Before we consider these processes, let us investigate the various properties of different waxes and how to use them.

Illus. 1. Bee collecting pollen.

Beeswax

Illus. 2. A honeycomb of virgin wax (left) next to a honeycomb of older wax. The difference can be recognized by comparing the light and dark shades.

Beeswax, which has always played a large role in liturgical functions of the Catholic Church, is a fatty substance which can be obtained through rendering (extraction by melting) of honeycombs. This kind of wax melts at temperatures of about 145 degrees F. It is soft, supple and pliant, becomes sticky when heated and has the unmistakable fragrance of honey. To obtain about 2 pounds of wax, bees would have to consume about fourteen times this weight in honey. Part of the bee's honey and pollen, when converted into wax inside the bee's body, is secreted in minuscule amounts under its rear-segment, and is stripped off with its hind legs to be utilized for the construction of the combs. Initially the wax is white and is referred to as pure wax.

Once formed into a beehive, the white honeycomb wax soon turns yellowish. The older the combs, the darker the color becomes. This explains

Illus. 2. A honeycomb of virgin wax (left) next to a honeycomb of older wax. The difference can be recognized by comparing the light and dark shades.

why genuine wax candles in stores frequently show a variation in color.

Since honey is more valuable than wax, it pays to save the bees a part of their work by hanging wooden-framed sheets of pure beeswax inside the hive. In this way the bees can immediately start stocking the cells with winter supplies and build them up for their larvae. The artificial honeycombs of beeswax are used also for the rolling of candles. They are obtainable from beekeepers, waxchandlers (candle dealers), honey wholesalers and hobby shops.

Bees not only build their own cells but cover any cracks and rough surfaces to stop all air currents and insects hostile to them from entering the hive. Perhaps you have wondered why bees often settle on resinous plants when everyone knows that no honey

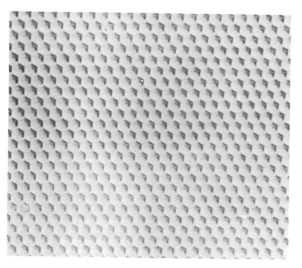

Illus. 3. A honeycomb sheet of pure wax. It can be used for rolling a candle or as the central wall of a hive.

can be extracted from them. But the bees do gather the resin, carry it to the hive and "plaster up" all the crevices. This resinous cement (propolis) must be blended with wax to become the glutinous wax which you will use for fastening the ornaments to your candles.

Illus. 4. A wooden hive frame. The central wall of beeswax is already hidden because the bees have begun cultivating their cells, and filling the cracks with a glutinous wax which is also used in candle-making.

Other
Waxes

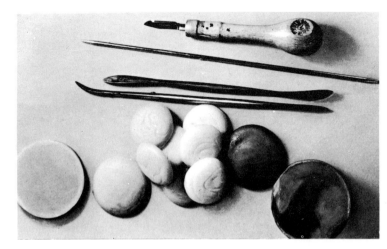

Illus. 5. (Top) Some of the tools used for wax moulding and incising. (Below) Moulding waxes of different shapes and shades.

Paraffin is a white, translucent, glasslike waxy substance distilled from petroleum. It has a low melting point. A candle made entirely of paraffin will drip considerably.

Hard paraffin melts at temperatures ranging from 125-158 degrees F. and its chief purpose is to serve as a supplementary addition to stearin and beeswax in the manufacture of candles. Soft paraffin wax can be melted at temperatures as low as 86 degrees F. It can be added to the wax mixture when the latter is supposed to be poured or pressed—either out of plaster of Paris casts or lino and wooden moulds. The malleable wax becomes even more elastic and flexible.

There are other waxes, such as earth wax or ceresin (melting point 170 degrees F.) or carnuba (melting point 196 degrees F.), which, when added to paraffin, tend to harden the mixture.

Tallow is made up of fatty animal tissue found in ox kidney suet, mutton drippings or goat fat, and it was used long ago for the manufacture of candles. Even today you can still find tallow candles in parts of Spain and other remote villages where farmers frequently make their own candles after the slaughter of cattle. Lime (calcium oxide) is added to the melted or rendered-down tallow and the lime absorbs all the impurities; next the tallow is carefully poured into a pot and cooked for about

7

Illus. 6. Working with candles requires the ut-most precision and concentration.

3 to 4 hours with vinegar. Candles made of tallow do have a greasy touch and a rather unpleasant, rancid odor. These disagreeable characteristics can be removed by a process of refinement.

Stearin (or more correctly stearic acid) is a soft, opaquely white, odorless solid which is made of natural animal and plant fats (palmitin). The melting point lies between 122 and 156 degrees F.; the stage where it becomes malleable is at about 120 degrees F. Adding paraffin to stearin will help in the casting of candles. Stearin candles burn well and do not bend as a result of the flame's heat.

Moulding wax is a combination of paraffin, stearin, with possibly a small addition of beeswax, and coloring and dyeing matter. You will need it in a hot, fluid, melted stage for the dipping of candles to imbue it with an even coating of color.

Modelling wax is a mixture of bleached beeswax and an equal amount of paraffin with dyes added to it. It is available in many colors.

Drop wax consists of collected remnants of wax, also leftovers of candles and candle-drippings. You can collect this kind of wax all year or get it at a low price from candlemakers.

Melt all these leftovers in water, in the process of which all impurities (soot, wicks, etc.) sink to the bottom of the hot water. They are left behind when the melted wax is carefully poured into another receptacle.

Wicks

Illus. 7. Various kinds of wicks in various strengths, waxed and unwaxed. The knot which signifies the "top" of the wick can be seen in the lower right-hand corner.

Wicks, the "souls" of candles, are manufactured from bleached cotton yarn in various thicknesses. The thicker the candle, the thicker the wick for it. Also the addition of beeswax plays a role when selecting a wick for its strength. For paraffin you would require the thinnest kind of wicks, for stearin medium-strong ones and the thickest wicks are reserved for beeswax candles. In other words, the circumference of the candle and the wax required for making it determine the thickness of the wick. It is advisable not to make your own wicks; you need much experience and a great instinctive flair for it, especially if you set out to have the wick end up at a certain thickness.

Finished wicks are obtainable in candle stores;

all you have to do is to mention the thickness of the candle and its components.

For "swaddled," or rolled up candles, and for thin, dip candles you might try to prepare your own wicks. Take some fine, bleached, not-too-coarse cotton yarn and twirl it into a cord consisting of four threads. You can also crochet a chain stitch, or braid a finely-honed "pigtail" of three threads.

To guarantee the right degree of flammability, dip the wick into a caustic made up of 2 per cent boric acid diluted in distilled water. When the wick is dry you proceed to dip it into wax and manipulate it from there.

The wicks you buy in stores are mostly spun wicks. These have a "bottom" and a "top." The top of the

Illus. 8. Some types of ornamentation require adding wax.

Illus. 9. Some types of ornamentation are performed by incising with a sharp tool.

wick is parallel with the top of the candle. Wax-chandlers indicate it with a knot because a layman would have difficulty seeing the difference between the unmarked top and bottom of wicks.

To color or dye the wax, you can buy dye that is soluble in fat in art supply shops. Obviously the more dye you add to the wax the deeper the color. These dyes are rich in color and are added to the fluid (melting) wax (or the paraffin-stearin composite).

Since it is not always easy to obtain such dyes you can also use colored wax crayons for this purpose, melting them in with the wax.

Illus. 10. (Left on opposite page) A candle in the process of being rolled or wrapped up. The wick has been pressed vertically into the edge on the short side of the beeswax sheet.

Illus. 11. (Right on opposite page) The finished rolled candle. You obtain the tapering conical contour by cutting the wax on top at a slant away from the wick.

Rolling Candles

The first method of making candles involves the wrapping or rolling of a honeycomb sheet of beeswax around a wick. With a pair of scissors, cut the wax sheet to the size you desire. Place the wax on a smooth base or surface. Press the wick vertically against the shorter side of the wax sheet and begin to roll the sheet around the wick. If you cut the wax on top at a slanting angle away from the wick, the shape of the candle will be enhanced by its tapering conical contour.

For a candle of about 6 inches in length you would cut a 12-inch wax sheet in half. The width of the sheet will determine the diameter of the candle. You will have to experiment with different widths to obtain various diameters. The wick should be about 1 inch longer than the height of the wax sheet.

A variation of this simple rolling process is to cut a rectangular wax sheet diagonally in half, place the wick on the longer side and roll up with great care.

The simple rolling of candles is devoid of all danger because in this case no wax has to be melted. Therefore it is possible to perform such a craft as early as kindergarten level.

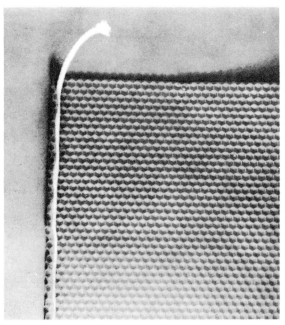

Dipping Candles

For candles made by dipping you need:

Beeswax, moulding wax, or a wax-paraffin mixture, wicks, a tall tin fruit can serving as a wax container, a saucepan for boiling water, and an electric hot plate or stove.

Put some wax into the fruit or vegetable can, place the can in a saucepan partially filled with water, and bring the wax to the point of melting by heating the water. Add a bit more wax to the can until the fluid wax almost fills the can. Stop only when you have reached a level one-half inch from the top of the container.

Now you dip a wick of about 40 inches in length into the fluid wax, pull it out again and let it hang— stretched taut—in the air until it solidifies. Then cut this piece up into several wicks, each about 2 inches longer than the height of the can. Quickly dip one of these pieces into the hot fluid, making sure it does not bend, and let it harden again. Repeat this procedure several times until you attain the required diameter. At the same time always replenish the substance of the hot wax in the can (which is diminished by the amount of wax absorbed by the wick) because otherwise the candle becomes increasingly thin at the top and too thick at the bottom. (Never use direct heat on wax as it is highly

a   c   b   d

Illus. 12. Candle dipping: (a) shows the wick after it has been dipped only once in wax; (b) is a wick dipped several times, but the candle is still soft and shapeless; (c) the candle has been straightened; (d) it has been cut into shape at the bottom with a heated knife.

flammable. If wax should break into flames, smother the fire with a tight metal cover—never use water to extinguish burning wax.)

You will note that if the wax is too hot it will not stick to the wick. You can turn off the heat or simply reduce the flame under the saucepan. It is also possible that you may have lingered too long dipping the wick in the wax; in the latter case, the wax that initially adhered to the wick will melt off.

Once you have mastered the dipping of candles, you still have to put them into shape. To start with, you straighten them. With a heated knife, cut off the thick bottom part of the candle where the wax has run down. Place the candle on a dampened glass or marble surface and roll it with the aid of a smooth wooden board or tray. Once the top of the wick has been shortened, the candle is finished.

You will notice that the dipping of candles is a time-consuming chore. It pays therefore to build your own device to make use of your time while the wax solidifies around the wick. Screw a few hooks into a ledge about 3¼ inches apart and tie the wicks to them (Illus. 13). This ledge or board should hang in such a way that no object obstructs your candle-making operations: it could be hung between two cupboards or two doorjambs. You can also fasten an overhanging ledge to a table with the aid of two clamps.

Tie the unwaxed wicks to these hooks. To make sure that the wicks hang down straight, attach a pearl or another weight to the bottom end of the wicks. Next melt some wax in a jug or container with a handle that is easy to grip. (Use the saucepan filled with water method.)

This time, however, do not dip the wick into the wax but reverse the procedure: raise the container

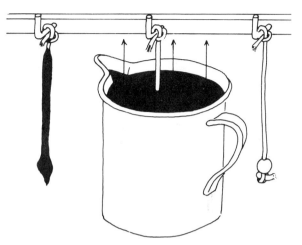

Illus. 13. How to set up a ledge with hooks for hanging wicks in the dipping process. The container with the hot fluid wax has been lifted.

to the wick. In this way you impregnate or saturate one wick after the other. Once you come to the end of the row of wicks you start again with the first one without waiting in between.

This candle-dipping can be performed on special occasions by a group of children at home or in school. Of course, everything has to be well-organized, carefully planned and thought through beforehand to prevent accidents with the hot wax as well as the soiling of clothes and the floor. Consequently each child should receive a wick (with the pearl weight already knotted into the other end), and a piece of cardboard to hold underneath the candle to prevent drippings on the floor. (Teachers particularly will be grateful to note how both hands of each child are fully occupied.)

The children stand in a line and slowly approach

the container with the hot wax, which is tended by the instructor or person in charge. Once a child has reached the container, he quickly dips the wick into the wax, pulls it out, holds the cardboard under the wick and proceeds on his pre-arranged course. After each child has had his turn eight or ten times in this fashion, the candles will have attained the right thickness. The children now return to the places at their tables and complete their chore. The cutting off is best left to the adult in charge.

This candle-making by a group of children can become a festive activity. The right mood can be achieved by a series of well-planned events: perhaps to start with, a visit to a waxchandler's, followed by the telling of a story in which the burning of a candle represents the light of life, next a song dealing with candlelight (the most appropriate of them being "O Tannenbaum"), or the preparation for working on candlesticks. This will stimulate the entire afternoon's activity.

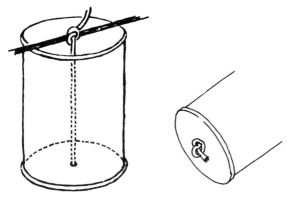

Moulding Candle Shafts

Illus. 14. This open-top fruit can with its taut wick fastened round a knitting needle is being prepared for pouring. The wick is knotted through a hole in the base.

For moulded candles you will require: Moulding wax, drippings of candles or a combination of stearin and paraffin (beeswax can be added). Cans of various sizes or plastic cups with completely vertical walls can serve as casting forms. You will also need: thick wicks, knitting needles for attaching the wicks, a pot for melting the wax, a saucepan for boiling water, a tray with cold water, and a stove.

Punch a hole with a nail into the middle of the bottom of an empty fruit can which has been thoroughly cleaned. Pull the wick through the hole. (In case you use plastic cups take a hot knitting needle to punch the hole.) Make a knot at the end of the wick to prevent it from sliding through the hole in the can. At the top, tie the wick to the middle of a knitting needle which you then place horizontally

over the rim of the can; see to it that the wick is as taut as possible without flexing the knitting needle. Place another fruit can filled with wax in the saucepan of water.

Bring the water in the saucepan to boiling, so that the wax in the fruit can reaches the melting point. Moisten the sides of the container you are using as

Illus. 15. The cans filled with wax stand in a tray of cold water to prevent the wax from seeping through the opening in the base.

a mould with water and pour in the melted wax. (Special effort must be made to prevent the wick from receiving any sprinkles of water so it will be saturated properly with wax.)

The moulding forms should be placed in an enamel tray of cold water before pouring the wax. That way very little wax can actually seep through the opening in the bottom of the container; in any case, the wax will solidify almost immediately and stop up the hole completely.

You will become aware after some time that a slight depression has formed around the wick; to level the wax you simply add a little more melted wax into the mould. You may even have to repeat this a second time. About 10 to 12 hours later (not earlier), you may pull the candle out of its cast.

First cut off the knot beneath the mould and then pull firmly at the wick, using the knitting needle to which it is tied as a lever. Should you not be able to remove the candle from its mould, leave the can for a short time in boiling water. In this way some of the hardened wax will melt from the walls of the mould and the candle will slide more easily out of its confines.

Due to this process of renewed melting, the shape of the candle will no longer be as smooth as it would have been otherwise. To remedy this, roll the candle back and forth as you did with your dipped candles on a marble or other equally smooth surface.

Candles made of previous candle drippings often show a muddy, opaque coloration. But there is a remedy for this too. Quickly dip your completed candle into some liquid moulding wax which has been poured into a deep container. The lighter the base color of the candle, the brighter the color of the new wax coating will appear.

Illus. 16. Candles made of layers of colored wax.

Multi-Layered Candles

To make multi-colored layer candles you will need: pouring wax in several colors, a transparent plastic cup serving as a cast or mould (the latter must tolerate heat up to 194 degrees F.) and all the other items required for the making of cast or poured candles.

Separate the various colors of pouring wax and melt each of them in its own container. Meantime, prepare a number of transparent plastic cups just as you did in the previous project, and place them in a tray of cold water. Start off with one color and pour a little bit into one of the cups. Once it has hardened, add an equal amount of wax of a different color. Continue like this until the cup has been filled. Do the same with the other cups. The results depend mainly on your sense of aestheticism in

Illus. 17. When the wax of a multi-layer candle becomes hard, a cavity forms around the wick. More wax has to be added—perhaps twice— until the top evens out.

tastefully arranging the colors required for making each candle. This will result in any number of variations. The outside stripes are, by virtue of their own coloration, so attractive that they are in no need of further embellishment.

Transparent plastic cups are most suitable for this purpose because they will enable you to control the amounts of wax poured as well as help you to determine the color composition of the individual candle. After your first attempt you will learn that the wax will have to be poured most carefully to avoid splashing the walls of the cup with liquid bits of wax which would show up on an upper layer of the candle. Remember, therefore, to pour the wax with great caution into the middle of the cup. After 10 or 12 hours, you can pull the candles out of the cups. They are easier to remove from plastic cups than from cans, and they are also smoother.

Nutshell Candles

Another interesting project is making nutshell candles.

Carefully halve shells of large walnuts. Bend some waxed wicks 1½ inches long at a right angle ¼ of an inch from the wick's end. Glue the small portion of the wick into the middle of the carefully emptied half of a nutshell so that a 1¼-inch piece of the wick stands up vertically in the shell. Now fill the shell with fluid wax. These little nutshell-boats should serve a unique purpose in midsummer festivals outdoors, as for instance by setting them afloat in a small pond or brook when the wind is calm. They can also be a most attractive table decoration, particularly on the occasion of a child's birthday party, if you place a number of these shells—lit—in a flat dish filled with some water.

Illus. 18.
Nutshell
candles
afloat.

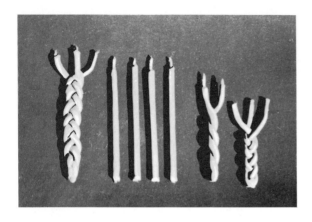

Tapers

Another form of candle-making involves winding a waxed wick around a core to obtain tapers of various shapes. It is not easy to do a truly attractive job of winding a waxed wick. It is advisable, therefore, to make a few simple attempts at winding wicks prior to launching a larger project. For this purpose use a thick piece of cord and dip it into fluid wax. Wind the cord while it is still pliable. As the core around which to wind the cord you can use, for example, a plastic or glass tube that contained pills.

The important thing to remember here is not to wind the cord haphazardly without any concern for beauty, but symmetrically, with the cord windings either lying close together or overlapping. The core can be removed after the work is completed. On the other hand, if the form has been completely covered it can remain inside the taper. Naturally in the latter case you would not use a fragile object but an appropriately formed piece of wood.

Illus. 20 shows a taper of the Biedermeier period (first half of the 19th century); it is actually an intricately lined wood block. Such tapers have often been preserved in breakfronts and hope chests as showpieces and even though wives have been proud of owning them they were virtually never lit.

Once you have practiced enough and feel that you have acquired a certain skill in winding such wicks, you can begin with the actual project at hand.

This time you melt the wax in a flat dish on top of a saucepan of boiling water. A thin wick about 40 inches long is held in both hands and slowly pulled through the wax (which will give you an idea why the wick should not be longer). Hang the wick straight down until it solidifies. Pick it up again and repeat the process of drawing it through the wax about three or four more times; by that time the taper should be thick enough.

This waxed cord, however, must be wound around your object while it is in a warm flexible state. Should the wax crack or break it means that it has cooled beyond its flexing state. You simply have to throw it back into the wax dish, melt it again and repeat the process. (See the small taper on the cover of this book.)

You can also use the cord method to create some small candles. Cut the waxed cord into pieces which you then roll on a smooth surface. Two or three such cords wound up or braided together will serve well as lights for a doll's house. (See Illus. 19.)

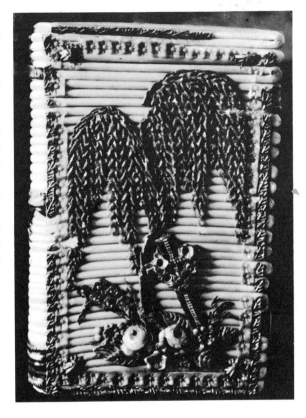

Illus. 20. A taper from the early 19th century.

Designing Ornamentation

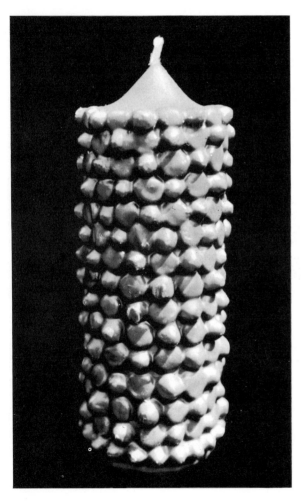

Now that you know the basics of candle-making, and after you have made a number of candles, you can go on to decorating your candles. The true artistic value of the candles you produce will lie in your perception and use of the intrinsic characteristics of wax.

Wax is a patient and amorphous material. It offers little resistance and is capable of performing many duties. You can press, shape, cut, color, glue, pull, melt or pour it. The way you shape it, it will remain. At the same time, these attractive characteristics conceal certain danger signals, particularly in the realm of taste.

Only in the final act of embellishing the candles will you reflect your own personal imprint on your candles and make their functional purpose unmistakably clear. In this connection it is sometimes unavoidable that problems arise which are influenced or determined both by the material (wax) and the purpose for which the candle is supposed to serve.

Just take a look at the highly decorative candles for sale in department and stationery stores, even at the waxchandler's. Many distasteful end products are offered. Some are especially distasteful if you

Illus. 21. A good example of simple unpretentious decoration of a candle's surface. Notice that alleyways are left for the drippings to travel downwards.

consider the functional purpose of the candle. To burn and shine brightly, a candle has to consume itself. The flame heats up the wax; the wax begins to melt. If this melting process does not eat up the candle itself, the wax trickles slowly down in droplets. For example, if you glue a head on a wax figure and it melts off, the figure becomes half-covered with dripping globules of wax—not a pretty sight.

A burning candle becomes warm, the wax soft. With deeply indented candles, you have to make certain that the downward path of the wax as it is consumed is not impeded and the candle does not bend.

Accordingly, you must regard a candle as you would a column, a pillar, and decorate it in such a way that it will never lose its over-all effect, whether looked at from in front or in its full circumference. On the whole, you should not launch projects using medallions or bouquets, or graphically dramatic scenes glued to one side of the candle, or deep one-sided incisions. *Suitable* ornamentation can enliven the smooth surface of the candle by means of impressions from modelled, whittled, or poured forms.

Another means of "animating" the candle's appearance, of course, is color. The symbolic nature of the color can point to the function of a candle's purpose.

White personifies purity, innocence, revival, and

religious renewal. (Baptismal, communion, Easter and altar candles.)

Red is the color of joy, life, love.

Green symbolizes new life, hope, understanding,

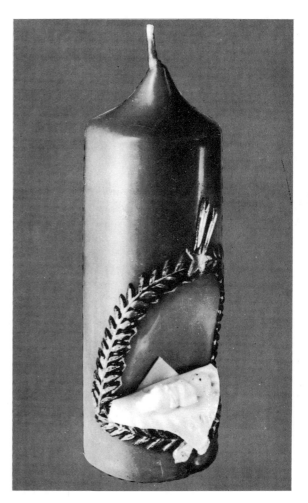

Illus. 22. An example of a tasteless form of candle. The deep incision near the base will cause the candle to bend as it is consumed, and besides it is pointless. Its religious theme tends to conflict with a candle's purpose—providing light. A better way to handle a religious theme is shown in Illus. 62.

Illus. 23. Spiral ridging with moulding wax.

growth. (White candles with green decorative motifs are most suitable for birthdays.)

Blue stands for loyalty and relationships. (Memorial and gift candles.)

Gold (honey-yellow) is a token of preciousness.

The moulding wax for your decorative purposes can be the same color as the candle's shaft; it can vary slightly in its shading or have totally different colors for contrast. On the following pages a number of ornamental techniques are suggested. The pictured examples are the works of children, teen-agers and adults; they were completed during art instruction classes and in their own leisure time. They represent various means of solving problems inherent in every project and are intended to stimulate the novice in designing his own ornamental shapes.

Illus. 24. Vertical ridging with moulding wax.

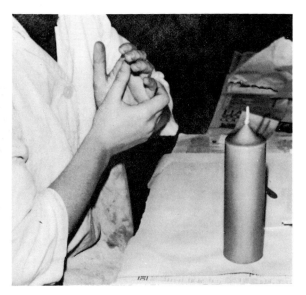

Illus. 25. Knead the moulding wax in your hands until it is pliable.

Illus. 26. If the moulding wax is cold, heat it in warm water, then roll it out on a glass plate.

Decorating
Candles

Your first attempts at candle decoration should be performed without the aid of any instrument. In this way you will somehow learn to respect the material you work with by manipulating it. Select a fat candle, preferably a candle stump, to avoid paying too much attention to the finer details of candle-making for the moment.

Either knead the moulding wax in your hands or place it in water no warmer than 104 degrees F. That way it will be uniformly soft and more pliable. Roll it with your hand on a smooth surface, such as a glass plate, until it emerges cord-like. This serves to provide you with a simple and basic form from which many varieties of ornamental figures can be forged: straight lines spaced equidistantly or un-

evenly, horizontally or vertically, serpentine lines, spirals of circular shapes, and many other designs can be pressed on the candle. Adding a touch of glutinous wax helps greatly in fixing your decorations to the candle's shaft. Another basic form, the dot or point (small wax balls) furnishes still further possibilities. Equal-sized points and those differing in size, round and flattened forms, clusters of two or more "dots" as well as multi-colored ones can be arranged by improvisation. You can vary spaces between decorations organizing them evenly or unevenly and so on. (For samples see Illus. 36 38, 47, 49, 51.)

Of course, balls and rope-like shapes are not the only wax ornaments at your command. The simple procedure of imprinting small objects (matchsticks, pencils, the tip of a knife) into the soft wax will produce attractive border designs which you then glue to the candle. (Illus. 30 and 31 show several ornamental border strips which have been prepared

Illus. 27. When you have shaped and pressed the moulding wax to the desired form, place it round the candle, and press it against the wax shaft with a heated iron tool or a moulding wood (see Illus. 28).

Illus. 28. Small punches of wood or plaster are useful for pressing ornamentation on to candle shafts, and also for imprinting their shape in the moulding wax. Cut the design into the head of the punch.

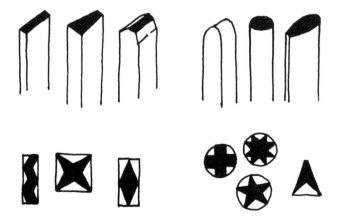

that way. The candle on the left of the cover is a completed wax-border project.)

A number of instruments will serve you well when melting wax decorations directly on to your candles, such as a steel knitting needle, a long nail, maybe a putty or palette knife or trowel or awl, an old pocketknife.

As usual, prepare your place of work. Lay everything out neatly on the surface on which the projects are to be executed and make sure it is clean and smooth. This time, light a candle which will come in handy for heating the tips of your tools.

The soft moulding wax must be rolled into thin strips to be placed on the candle. This time glueing the wax is not necessary because in this melting technique the wax cords can be pressed on to the candle with the aid of the metal tools which you have previously heated in the other candle's flame. As a consequence the wax will show some grooves or indentations, visible traces where the wax ornament has been melted on to the candle. At the

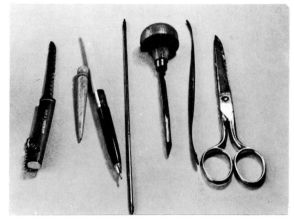

Illus. 29. A few of the metal instruments you can use for pressing and melting wax decorations on to your candle shafts.

same time additional traces or marks of coloring will be left behind by the metal that has gotten lightly caked with soot from the candle's flame.

Illus. 30. These wax border decorations were made in moulding wax by pencil points, folded edges or the tip of a scissors.

Illus. 31. Tiny wax rosettes made with the tip of a matchstick and a knife.

This, however, will help in emphasizing the top layer's surface structure. The metal becomes especially black if you hold it directly above the flame, but hardly at all if held in it (something that might bring back memories of your physics lessons). The second candle on the left of this book's cover was completed in this fashion. In addition to the above process, moulding waxes in a number of colors—a light moss green, light and dark honey shades and a bright brown—were used.

The strips of wax were placed around the candle, starting at the bottom, but with each successive border varying in color from the one directly below it. The candle shown immediately to the right of it (in the back row) also represents a wax-melted project; here the decorative pattern is that of small pre-formed wax scales.

Illus. 32. Decorated candles made by 11-year-old students.

Gallery of Ornamented Candles

In this gallery of candles a number of techniques of ornamentation are suggested by the photographs. They are intended to stimulate your own creative ideas, and are not for copying. Each shows how a particular problem was solved.

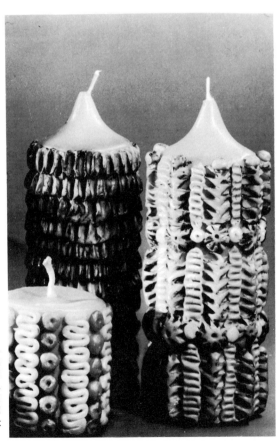

Illus. 33. Three candles representing different techniques. The small candle shows hand-formed ornaments. The dark candle in the background demonstrates the melted-on pattern of tiny forms, and the candle on the right displays multi-colored strips and dots of wax which have been grouped with care on the candle's shaft and pressed on it with the heated tip of a scissors.

Illus. 34. Free-form ornaments.

Illus. 35. Punched ornaments.

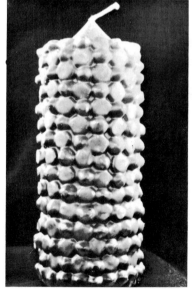

Illus. 36. Dot clusters.

Illus. 37. Close-up
of dot clusters.

Illus. 38. Holes in
dots made by pencil
point.

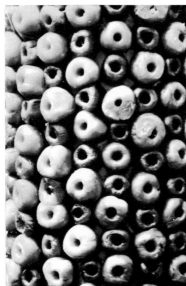

Illus. 39. Close-up
of holed dots.

Illus. 40. Concentric rings of moulding wax.

Illus. 41. Rope-like rosebuds lined up.

Illus. 42. Free-form hearts.

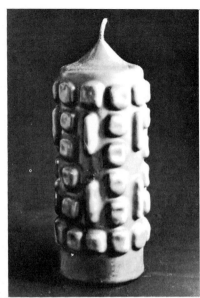

Illus. 43. Hand-moulded cubes.

Illus. 44. Dot-on-dot projections.

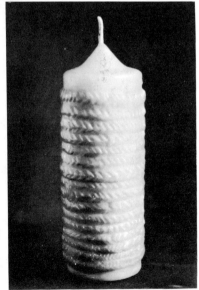

Illus. 45. A ringed cord effect.

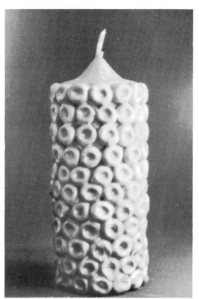

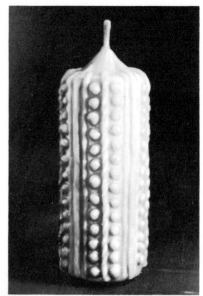

Illus. 46. Life savers.

Illus. 47. Dots in random fashion.

Illus. 48. Vertical border strips.

Illus. 49. Large dots moulded on.

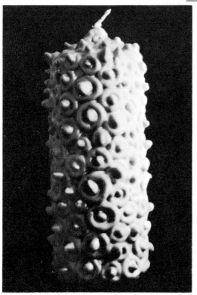

Illus. 50. Combination of holed and projecting dots.

Illus. 51. Small joined dots in alternate rows.

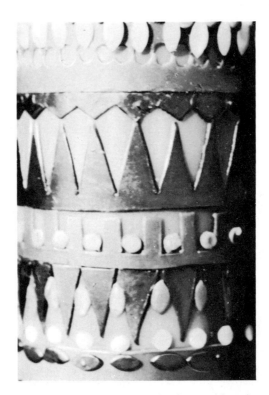

Illus. 52. Ornamentation made from colored wax
sheets cut into geometric shapes joined together.
See finished candle in Illus. 53.

Geometric Designs

from Wax Sheets

Another method of decorating candles is using geometric designs cut from purchased or self-poured wax sheets made of moulding wax. You will need a number of cutting tools such as nail scissors, silhouette scissors, and knives, as well as a ruler, a pane of glass, and machine oil.

First the moulding wax is melted via the can-in-boiling-water method. Then it is poured on an oiled pane of glass. Frame the glass with plasticine sticks to prevent the wax from running over the edge of the glass. After the wax has hardened, but while it is still in a soft, flexible condition, remove the sheet for further treatment.

First cut the sheet into small geometric forms that can be pressed on the candle for decorative purposes. Since in this particular case the pieces are thin and small, a simple pressure with your thumb will suffice. The charm of the decoration is enhanced by the different colors of the wax and the rhythmic grouping or arrangement of the wax forms.

You can perhaps save yourself the effort of pouring the wax by carefully pressing and pulling the moulding wax with a rolling pin, but this "time saver" frequently results in an uneven thickness of the wax sheet.

Illus. 53. The completed candle is made doubly effective by its vivid colors.

Cut-Out Designs

For another type of decoration you must cut out your patterns to start with. For your design patterns you may use linoleum, plaster of Paris or wood. We will not discuss wood cutting in further detail because, on the one hand, working with wood requires some previous experience and an artisan's dexterity while, on the other hand, the linoblock or the plaster of Paris cut can serve as preparation for future woodwork.

When designing your pattern always take into consideration the circumference and length of the candle. It is advisable therefore to cut out a paper model conforming with the girth of the candle and sketch your patterns and their grouping into it prior to starting on your linocut design. So you can follow the drawing and incision more clearly, coat the linoleum with a white body color. After you have pencilled in your design, the cutting process can begin. The incisions must be done forcefully, clearly and deeply. The impressions of the linocut are

Illus. 54. Press the wax hard on to the linoleum (right). The impression of the linocut will be left fairly sharp and clean in the wax. Cut it out (left) and it is ready for glueing on the shaft. (See Illus. 55.)

transferred to the soft, drawn-out wax once you press it into the incision.

Now is the time to make any necessary corrections you feel have to be undertaken. Once you are content with the imprint, the wax surrounding the pattern has to be cut along the decoration's edge. Finally, you fasten the ornament to the candle with some glutinous wax. But be careful not to press too hard, otherwise you run the danger of flattening the design, making the three-dimensional impressions invisible.

The pulling and pressing of wax sheets is not simple. Always hold the sheet of wax against the light to see that it is even in its thickness and all kinks have been "ironed out."

Basically you will have to apply the same principles to plaster of Paris moulds as you did in the case of linocuts. The soft wax is also pressed into the moulded, carved-out form. However the plaster mould leaves behind a much more pronounced and precise contour than does the linoleum. (Compare Illus. 55 with Illus. 58.) This must be taken into account as well as exploited when designing your pattern.

Before embarking on your design you have to prepare your slab of plaster of Paris. An old enamel dish, a large empty fruit can or a plastic bucket are most suitable for this purpose. The container should be about half full of water and the plaster carefully added (in the proportion of 1:1) until a small mound of it turns up on the surface of the water (see Illus. 57a). Mix the combination of water and plaster slowly, because a hasty stirring will result in mixing air into the mass, the effect of which will show up in some quite unattractive little holes in the plaster. Next pour the mass into the frame. This

Illus. 55. The completed candle with pine-tree ornaments made from linocuts.

Illus. 56. A birthday candle made from linocut ornaments.

consists of four wooden boards nailed together which have previously been well-lathered with soft soap and placed on a pane of glass (see Illus. 57b). The plaster of Paris grows warm after a time and then cools again. This is when it becomes solid and can be lifted out of its wooden form. Now is the moment to cut the plaster to its right size With the point of a knife press along the edge of a ruler, tracing a line back and forth where you want the border to be, and then break off the superfluous part of the plaster on the edge of a table.

The wax decorations can be laid in small pieces (Illus. 58), in strips (Illus. 61) or as a complete encircling coat around the candle. As before, you will have to determine the candle's circumference for your design. To do this make use of a paper template and wind it around the candle. Note though that the candle's circumference increases with the thickness of the wax impression. Also the glutinous wax required for fastening the ornamentation adds to the girth. It is better to have the wax design a trifle too large than too small, as this is not so conspicuous. Moreover you can cut a small strip off your over-large applied coat if it does not affect the design too much.

Let the plaster of Paris dry another day. Create and transfer the design, possibly in reverse (as in the case of letters), to the plaster. Only then can you actually start with the scratching, scraping and cutting out of the design. First, try out your cutting tools on a scrap of the hardened plaster to determine which tools are most suitable for your various designs.

When the design is carved, press a flattened wax sheet on the completed plaster of Paris form from which all the gypsum dust and particles have been thoroughly removed. Any wax showing beyond the edge of the plaster-design borders must be cut off with a pair of scissors or a knife.

It is quite hard to press a coat evenly around a large candle. For such an occasion it is better to carve the complete design on a large plaster slab and pour melted wax into the plaster form. This process is described on the next page.

Illus. 57a. To make plaster of Paris, add the plaster to the container of water (proportion 1:1) until the mound of plaster shows above the surface of the water.

Illus. 57b. The frame for plaster casts must be rubbed with soft soap before receiving the plaster, and should be placed on a plate of glass.

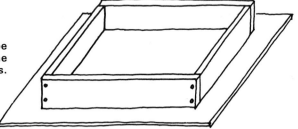

Illus. 58. The plaster-cast wax design fits perfectly round this candle.

Finishing Plaster-Cast Wax Moulds

After carving the design, you coat the mould with shellac that has been diluted with alcohol. This causes the form to lose its delicateness.

When the shellac has dried, brush some oil over it or wet it. Place a frame-like structure of plasticine sticks around the form to prevent the overflow of the wax. For this pouring project you need liquid moulding wax to which some soft paraffin has been added. (Mixture: 3 parts liquid wax, 1 part soft paraffin and a few drops of Venetian turpentine.) However, since liquid moulding wax is supplied by different manufacturers in various combinations always make sure that the right amount of soft paraffin is added.

The purpose of this mixture is to make the wax more flexible, or elastic, to be able later to raise the poured mass out of its flat mould without cracking it. The process of lifting it from the form must occur the moment the wax begins to solidify but while it is still warm. Should the design show a crack anywhere it would require an additional amount of soft paraffin. If, on the other hand, the wax is too greasy, it means that too much turpentine has been added. After coating the backside with glutinous wax, apply the design around the candle and press it gently. The seam where the two ends of the design meet has to be filled in or plastered up with a hot knife.

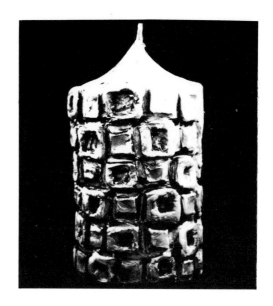

Illus. 59. Soot-traces help to emphasize the outlines of this design.

You will have noticed while applying your decorations to the candle's shaft that the inadvertently formed soot-traces helped to emphasize and reinforce the outlines of your design. This is an experience you should exploit to the fullest. The poured wax coat may appear quite flat in its decorative design but you can accentuate it.

This can be achieved by blackening with powdered graphite or lead. Any excess or smears of soot can be dabbed away with a piece of soft cloth dipped in turpentine so that the only black reinforcement lines visible are those in the wax-design depressions and indentations.

Designs from
Plaster-Cast
Wax Moulds

Illus. 60. A small plaster of Paris casting and next to it a candle with the moulded design attached.

Illus. 61. A full encircling coat of wax was poured for this candle into a plaster form.

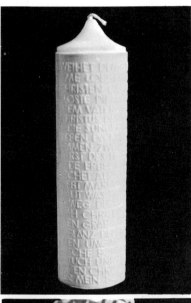

Illus. 62. This baptismal candle is most effective because of the simplicity of its lettering.

Illus. 64. A combination of lettering and figures in an aesthetic handling of a religious theme.

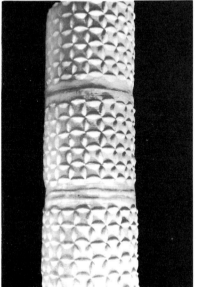

Illus. 63. A wax ribbon poured from the same plaster mould has been arranged decoratively in three tiers.

Illus. 65. A badly calculated design. A gap has been left in wrapping the mould round the shaft. This could be due to failure to allow for the thickness of the mould and the glutinous wax. The gap can be filled in with a hot knife.

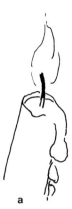

Illus. 66.

Checklist

You must know how to treat a candle:

a. Candles must stand vertically upright, so they never burn off and drip sideways.

b. Strong currents of air and draughts also tend to cause heavy dripping to one side.

c. Always let a new candle burn at first until the whole candle top has been filled up with liquid wax; otherwise, the top will show an ungainly wall.

d. Walls produced in this manner should be gently pressed in toward the middle of the candle.

e. A candle with a long wick causes soot; it helps therefore to cut back the wick from time to time.

f. When extinguishing the flame, dip the wick into the liquid wax and right it again to prevent sooting and smoking.

☐ Never break off the charred end of a wick prior to lighting the candle because you will have difficulty lighting it.

a

b

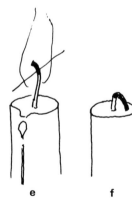

c   d   e   f

Naturally the candles which you made with so much effort and devotion need a suitable holder.

Basically, this can be said: The shape of a candle holder must be in accord with its purpose. The holder has to serve the candle. Its primary missions are to catch the wax, to hold the candle up and to give it a firm support. Consequently such holders require a tray for catching wax drippings, a stem for impaling the candle and a base. How low or high the stem should be placed depends on the candle's function. For home use a short stem is sufficient; you can even do without any elevated base. Heavily decorated candles should have a plain holder in order not to detract from the candle.

For plain candles a more elaborate candlestick can be used, such as the ones shown in another book of this series, *Nail Sculpture*, a study of how to create, among other useful and decorative objects, different candlesticks of soldered nails.

Index